이명희 시집
The Collection of Myung Hee Lee's Poems

한영대역판
*Korean-English Edition*

# 이브여, 눈을 뜨라

# EVE, OPEN YOUR EYES

이 명 희
Myung Hee Lee

이명희 시집
The Collection of Myung Hee Lee's Poems

한영대역판
*Korean-English Edition*

# 이브여, 눈을 뜨라

# EVE, OPEN YOUR EYES

이 명 희
Myung Hee Lee

도서출판 두손컴
Doosoncomm Publishing Co. Book

# 서문

아침마다 일어나 집안일을 다 해놓고 가야 할 곳이 있어 마냥 바쁘기만 하다. 수년 동안 어려움을 극복하며 만든 자그마한 일터에는 몇 안 되는 직원들이 나를 쳐다보고 개미같이 일을 한다. 대부분이 여성으로 구성되어 있어서 마음으로 통하는 일이 많다. 역시 손님들도 여성이어서 사뭇 웃음으로 시간을 보내기가 일쑤다. 그렇지만 아무리 바빠도 우리의 생활 속에서 아름답고 보람 있는 생활을 추구하기 위하여 시간이 있을 때마다 조금씩 조금씩 나의 마음을 모아둔 것을 시집으로 내게 된 것이 큰 보람된 일이 아닐 수 없다. 물론 누구에게나 익숙하게 읽혀질 시로서는 부족함이 많을 줄 안다. 그러나 나에게는 또 다른 세계로 첫발을 내딛는다는 것이 그저 기쁨으로 다가올 뿐이다. 우리들이 가지는 일상생활에서 듣고 보고 생각하는 것을 글로써 나타내고 싶었던 것이 항상 나의 바람이었기 때문이다. 좀 더 어릴 때 이런 기회가 있었다면 지금보다 더 행복했을지도 모른다.

# Preface

Every morning I was busy because I had to do all the housework after I woke up, and had to go somewhere. At my small place of work that I made by overcoming difficulties for several years, the few employees look at me and work like ants. Most of them are women so I can really communicate with them. Most customers are women as well, so I spend many times laughing. It is a great fulfillment for me to publish this book of poems that I gathered bit by bit, whenever I had the luxury to, in order to pursue a beautiful and fulfilling life no matter how busy life becomes. I am well aware that for many people, it might be lacking in some ways, as compared to those poems that are read with familiarity. However, it is just true happiness for me to be able to take a step into an entirely new world. It was always my wish to write what I heard, saw and thought in daily life. I may have been happier if I had such opportunity when I was younger.

시간은 우리를 기다려 주지 않지만, 나는 이 시간을 얼마나 기다렸는지 모른다. 비록 아무도 알아주지 않는 것이라 할지라도, 이렇게 하여 곱게 곱게 살고 싶다. 육체적 피곤하거나 정신적으로 피곤한 여성들이 좌훈을 하려 나의 일터에 와서 일일이 들려주는 재미있는 이야기가 앞으로 좀 더 아름다운 글로서 태어났으면 한다. 그래서 일차적으로 이 시집의 제목을 "이브여, 눈을 뜨라"고 만들어 보았다. 이제 여성들의 사회참여가 많아지고 좋은 역량을 아낌없이 발휘하는 것을 볼 때 기쁘기 한이 없다. 나도 분명, 한 사람의 여인으로서 눈을 뜨고 싶다. 저어 아름다운 시의 나라로…….

2014년 초여름

이 명 희

Time does not wait for us, but I waited very long for this time. Even if I am not acknowledged, I would like to live in the peace that poetry brings me. I hope that I can give new birth through beautiful words, to the interesting stories that women who are physically or mentally exhausted tell me, as they come for hip fumigation. That is why I titled this collection of poems, "Eve, Open Your Eyes". I rejoice when I see many women taking part in society and utilizing their many great talents. I, too, wish to open my eyes as a woman... in that beautiful world of poetry.

Early Summer, 2014

Myung Hee Lee

## 저자소개 About the Author

- (주)캄리 대표이사
- 고려대학교 경영전문대학원 교우회 이사
- 한중친선협회 이사
- 새부산시인협회 회원
- 국제라이온스 355-D 지구 여명 L/C 이사

- CEO, COMELY CO., LTD
- Director, Korea University Bussiness Management Alumni Association
- Director, The Korea-China Friendship Association
- A member, Poet Society of New Busan
- Director, International Association of 355-D Yeo Myeong Lions Clubs

| 목차 |

| 목차 |

## 이브여, 눈을 뜨라

잠들어 꿈꾸기조차 어려워
우리는 주어진 틀 속에서 살았고
신음은 어두운 밤하늘에서 떠날 줄 몰랐다

차가운 옷을 벗고
속박에서 벗어나는 새싹들
저기, 몸을 녹일 훈훈한 바람이 있구나

벌써 봄은 지나고 여름인데
욕망의 굴레를 어느 전쟁터에서 얻은 전리품처럼
허리에 동여매고 살아야 하는 조작된 행복

이제,
바람이 치마를 펄럭이게 하고
뜨거운 태양은 그대들의 옷을 벗게 하나니
이브여, 눈을 뜨라

다가오는 가을에 결실을 위해
환희여 빛깔로 아끼고, 사랑하자
이브여, 눈을 뜨라

# Eve, Open Your Eyes

Too hard to dream while sleeping
we live in a frame given unto us,
and moans know not how to leave the dark night sky.

Taking off their cold clothes,
shoots emerge from their shackles,
and there, warm wind to melt the body comes.

Spring has passed and it is summer,
but the restraints of desires are like spoils of war,
which are tied around our waists as fabricated happiness.

Now,
the wind flaps the skirt,
and the hot sun undresses you, so
Eve, open your eyes.

For the fruits of the coming autumn,
joy, save your colors and love,
Eve, open your eyes.

# 치마

아무리 가려도 걸어낸다
아랫도리는 멋대로 밖으로 뛰쳐나온다.
바람에 나부끼는 폭넓은 깃발
나의 부끄러움을 모른다

치맛바람 펄럭일 때마다
오므렸다 펴졌다 하는 펄럭이는 쾌감
신이 내려준 나의 만족이다

때로는 찢겨지고 닳아버리는
손수건보다 못하지만
돛단배에 매달린 깃발처럼
내가 항해하는 바다 같기도 하다

차라리 벗어 버리면 좋으련만
나를 풍요롭게 하는 치마
아름답게 펄럭인다.

# Skirt

No matter how much I cover it, it skims,
the bottom runs outside,
the wide flag that flutters in the wind,
it knows not my shyness.

Whenever my skirt flutters,
the joy of the fluttering that puckers and spreads,
it is my satisfaction given by god.

Sometimes it rips and becomes worn out,
and it is no better than a handkerchief,
like a flag hung on a sailboat,
it is like the sea that I navigate.

It might be nicer to just take it off,
but the skirt makes me fuller,
and it flutters beautifully.

# 투병 속의 어머니 손길

긴 겨울 외투 하나 없이 찬비 맞으며
아무리 나의 상흔을 어루만져도
지워지지 않는 육신

가냘픈 엄마는 내 곁에서 울어도
쉽지 않은 칙칙한 장마만
침실을 메운다.

어머니의 입가에는 주름이 잡혀도
입김으로 호호 불어주던 사랑은
나의 가슴에 움츠렸던 생명이 피어난다

먹구름 지나고 흐르는 신비의 서광
나의 구석구석 밝혀주셨던 정성
지금 내가 다시 어머니가 된다.

# Mother's Touch in Sickness

Being hit by cold rain without one coat in the long winter,
no matter how much my wounds are cared for,
the body does not erase.

Even if my feeble mother cries next to me,
the difficult and gloomy monsoon
fills my room.

Even if there are wrinkles around the mouth of my mother,
the love she blew into me
gives birth to life in my bosom.

A mysterious sign that flows after the dark clouds,
the devotion that brightened every corner of my body,
I now become a mother.

# 삶의 열정

움직이는 물결의 소용돌이인가
심저에 솟아나는 분수리던가
끝없는 하늘로 솟구쳐 오른다

정연, 푸르게 살아야 하기에
이토록 추운 겨울 무딘 인내로
기다려야 하는 뭉게구름

땅 위에 구르는 마른 잎이 애처로워
푸른 새잎이 하늘로 돋아나
태양을 정열로 받아들인다

날개 달지 않은 삶
저 앞에 떨어져 소멸될 것 알면서도
끝없는 날갯짓을 하고 있다.
오늘도, 내일도.

## Passion of Life

It is a whirlpool of moving water,
it is a fountain that shoots up from the bottom of one's heart,
whatever it is, it shoots up endlessly into the skies.

Because it must live blue,
through dull patience in such a cold winter,
cumulus will have to wait.

The dry leaves that roll on the land are pitiful,
so the new green leaves grow towards the skies,
and receive the sun with passion.

A wingless life,
knowing that it will fall and disappear right in front,
it ceaselessly flaps its wings.
Today, and tomorrow.

# 서러운 인연

사랑으로 엮을 줄 알았던 새끼줄이
이렇게 고독한 끈이 될 줄이야
마디마디 질시의 눈을 매달아 놓고
울타리에 걸쳐 놓는다

검은 눈이 내린다
공해에 찌든 삶이 베여있는 눈은
황토물처럼 금방 녹아내린다

나의 육신을 담그면
산화되어 하얗게 세탁될 줄 알았건만
잿빛 고독만 얼룩으로 남는다

고독은 서러움만 남기고
흐르는 강물 따라
파도 이는 바다로 간다

# Sad Relationship

This straw rope that I thought would tie with love,
I knew not that it would become such a lonely string.
Eyes of jealousy are tied on each knot
and placed on a fence.

Black snow falls.
The snow containing the life tainted with pollution
melts quickly like mud.

By soaking my body,
I thought it would oxidize and become clean,
but only ashy loneliness remain as spots.

Loneliness leaves sadness,
and like the flowing river water,
it goes to the seas filled with waves.

# 어머니의 거울

아침마다 쳐다보는 거울에
어머니가 없다

유달리 양 볼을 붉히던 다홍빛 모습
내 생각에 남아 있는데
거울을 보는 어머니의 옛 모습이 아니다

내 가슴에는 어머니 옛 모습
그대로 있었는데 거울 속을 아무리
찾아도 옛 어머니가 없다

허옇게 돋아나는 머리칼
모습은 애잔한 슬픔이 강물처럼 흐르고
눈가에 주름살은 이슬조차 말랐다

한평생 보듬어 안아주던
가슴은 앙상하게 말라
거친 손을 쓰다듬는 어머니 손길만
거울에 비쳐진다

# Mother's Mirror

In the mirror I look at every morning,
mother is not there.

Her scarlet cheeks,
still remain in my memory,
but it is not what my mother looked like in the past.

My mother's image in the past,
it was still there, but no matter how hard I look,
my mother is not in the mirror.

Her white hair,
her loving sadness flows like the river,
and even the dew on her wrinkles around her eyes, are dry.

Her breasts that caressed me for a lifetime
have thinned away,
and only mother's hand that strokes the rough hands
can be seen in the mirror.

그래도 인자한 미소만은 지울 수 없어
어느새 나는 어머니의 거울이 된다.

But the generous smile goes nowhere,
and I become my mother's mirror.

# 일개미

정신없이 일어나 거울 볼 틈 없이
온갖 체력 짜내고
시간도 짜내고
설익은 밥을 차리고
새끼들을 먹여야 어미 노릇이라고
책망한다, 나를

사무실 나가면 나를 기다리는 사람들
자식보다 더 또렷한
눈으로 나를 바라본다
일개미를

산더미 같은 흙을 잘게 부셔
한입씩 물고 나르는 개미의 신데
곧 지쳐버릴까 안쓰럽고
하루가 저물기 전에 일 마치기 하는
일개미가 안쓰럽다.

등에 붙은 가난의 멍에를 짊어져도
울 줄도 웃을 줄도 모르는
로봇이 부럽다 일개미는

## Worker Ant

Waking up in a hurry and unable to look in the mirror,
using all my strength,
using all my time,
I prepare half-cooked rice,
thinking that a mother should feed her children,
and I rebuke, myself.

The people who wait for me in the office,
with eyes clearer than my children's
they look at me,
a worker ant.

Mincing a mountain of dirt,
this is a poem about an ant that carries one at a time.
But I feel sorry for it that it might just become too exhausted.
I feel pity for the ant
that has to complete its work before the day ends.

Even if it carries the yoke of poverty attached to its back,
it does not know how to cry or laugh.
It envies robots, the worker ant.

# 붉은 감

시골의 한적한 정원에
붉은 감이 영글었다

가지가 무거워 애통을 해도
무심히 지나치는 주인이 원망스럽다

까치조차 마음을 주지 않고
다른 나무에서 물끄러미 바라만 본다

저 붉은 마음 한 하나
누구를 위함일까

붉은 열매 속에
용광로보다 더 뜨거운 정념이 있다.

# Red Persimmon

In a quiet garden in the country side,
a red persimmon is ripe.

The branch cries because of the heavy branch,
and it resents the owner for ignoring it.

Even a magpie gives it little attention,
and just stares from another tree.

That red heart,
who is it for?

In the red fruit
is a passion hotter than a furnace.

# 봄의 향연

소녀의 입김에 수줍음이 서려
아지랑이의 마음을 살랑거리게 하는데
뾰족이 내미는 새싹의 얼굴은
잠에 어리어 눈을 비빈다

말라버린 영혼에 생기가 돌고
그리움은 잠에서 깨어나
푸른 하늘의 구름을 바라본다

익숙지 못한 음성으로 노래하는 새들
어미는 안타깝게 맴돌지만
봄은 능성까지 올라와 나무들을 깨운다

온 산과 들은 이제 어우러져
파티복을 입고 심포니에 맞추어
봄의 왈츠를 춘다.

# Feast of Spring

There is bashfulness in the breath of a girl.
The heart of the haze flutters the heart,
but the face of a shoot that looks out sharply,
rubs its eyes, still not fully awakened.

Life circulates in a dried soul
and longing wakes from a slumber
and looks to the clouds in the blue sky.

Birds that sing with unfamiliar notes,
the mother circles around it with pity,
but spring rises to the ridges and awakens the trees.

The mountains and fields come together
and wearing the party dresses, and to the symphony,
they dance a waltz of the spring.

# 도심의 물결

도심은 진종일 열병을 앓는다
스피커는 도로를 흔들고
춤은 길을 메우고
사람들의 목가에 핏대를 세운다

무섭다
위기가 온 듯하다
보이는 것은 전무 절망이고
믿는 마음들은 송두리째 바람으로 날린다.

도심은 공해의 물결이다
지나가는 위선의 겸손으로
권력을 잡으려는
험난한 장애물 경기

호기심 반
걱정 반
합하면 하나지만
줄곧 도심은 몸살을 앓는다
편안한 곳 못 찾아
나도 몸살을 앓는다.

# Urban Waves

The city suffers from fevers all day long.
Speakers shake the streets,
dance fills the roads,
and veins pop out of the necks of people.

It is frightening.
A crisis has come.
What is visible is despair,
and faithful hearts are taken away by the wind.

The city is a wave of pollution.
With humility of passing hypocrisy,
a tough game
to gain power.

Half curious,
half worry,
the sum is one.
The city always suffers from aches.
Unable to find a place of refuge,
I am also filled with aches.

# 회상回想

하늘에 떠 있는
무지개 하나

님으로 내려와
풀잎에 앉으면
피는 꽃송이

어느새
열매 맺어 익어 가는데

세월의 몸부림에
저녁놀이 짙다

# Reminiscence

Floating on the sky
A rainbow

Comes down as a lover
To sit on a blade of grass
Then flowers bloom

Before we know it
Fruits are borne and ripened

Due to the struggle of time
The evening glow is thick

# 코드(암호暗號)

너무나 정확한 유전정보이기에
아비를 닮아야 바른 코드지
남의 아비 닮으면 잘못된 코드

아무리 다문화 사회가 된들
같은 민족, 같은 문화
함께 누리며

모두가 이해하며 살아가건만
극단極端의 틀린 코드 지닌 군상은
한심한 선량善良

한 때는 코드가 안 맞으면
세상을 활보하기 힘들더니만
이제는 완전히 두 종족이구나

암 유전자의 코드가 끼어들었나
우리들 눈에 비친 병든 종족들
의술로 유전자를 수선할 수 없을까?

# Code

Since genetic codes are so accurate
The codes are correct only when children resemble their father
And if they resemble someone else's father, the codes are wrong

No matter how much the society become multi-cultural
The same race enjoys
The same culture

And everybody lives understanding each other, but
The groups of people that have extremely different codes are
Pathetic elites

Once they said that if codes are not the same
It would be difficult to stride in the world
Now, they are two completely different races

Have the codes of cancer genes cut in?
Diseased races that are seen to our eyes
Can genes be repaired by medical techniques?

# 아린 가슴

그댈 사랑함은
사랑한다 말 못하기 때문입니다

세월이 내 곁에 머물 수 없기에
가슴에 그냥 묻어 둘 수 없었습니다.

아린 상처 깊게 하는
아둔한 나

먼 후일 만나면
사랑할 수 없다고 말해주세요

# Aching Heart

I love you
Because I cannot say that I love you

Since time cannot stay beside me
I could not keep it buried in my heart.

Deepening the aching wound
I am stupid

In the distant future, if you meet me
Tell me that you cannot love me

# 서러움

믿으려 해도 믿기지 않아
서럽습니다

자꾸만 생각나는
괴로운 몽상夢想

종기라면 짜버리고 싶은
서러움

주체 못 한 마음에
나의 영혼은 눈이 멀었습니다

# Sorrow

Unbelievable even though I try to believe and thus
I am sad

Repeatedly reminded
The painful fantasy

Sorrow
That I would like squeeze if it was a boil

Due to the uncontrollable mind
My soul has become blind

# 잃어버린 마음

별이 잠잘까 조바심만 숨 쉬는
고요한 이 밤

바람은 내 가슴을 뻥 뚫고 지나가는데
어둠을 껴안고 가식假飾의 춤을 춘다

심장이 없어 고동鼓動도 없다
달린 머릿속에 뇌마저 농膿해버렸다

겨우 로봇 춤을 춘다
모든 에너지는 소진消盡 되었다

이제, 괴로움마저 못 느끼는
처절한 식물인간이 됐다

# Lost Mind

Only anxiety breathes fearing that stars may sleep
At this silent night

Wind pushes through my mind but
I do a dance of false pretenses embracing darkness

There is no heart and thus there is no pulsation either
Even the brain in the head attached to the body has festered

I managed to do a robot dance
All energy was exhausted

Now, I have become a sorrowful human vegetable
That cannot even feel pain

# 잠 못 이루는 밤

밤이 두렵습니다
몹쓸 꿈속을 헤매게 될까
여명黎明이 영영 오지 못할까

밤이 두렵습니다
그대, 다른 정원에 서성여서
못 보게 되지나 않을까

밤이 두렵습니다
어두운 밤이
내 마음에 묻을까 두렵습니다.

# Sleepless Night

I am afraid of the night.
Perhaps I will wander in a terrible dream,
Perhaps dawn will never come.

I am afraid of the night.
You, might pace around in another garden,
and I might not be able to see you.

I am afraid of the night.
Perhaps the dark night,
will close my heart.

# 어느 슬픈 날

밤하늘에 하얀 깃털 가진 구름은
달을 품고 흐르는데
빈 내 가슴, 무엇을 품을까

구름에 모아둔 그리운 언어로
그대의 꿈속에
달빛으로 내릴까, 별빛으로 내릴까

내릴 곳 잃어버린 무거운 절망에
눈물로 빈 가슴 채워
길가에 주저앉은 육신

옮기는 빈 걸음은
세월 따라 걷는데
빈 낙엽 위에 가을이 외롭다

# A Sad Day

The clouds with white feathers in the night sky
Flowed and embraced the moon
What shall my empty heart embrace?

With the language of longing gathered in the clouds
In your dream
Shall I ride the moonlight or starlight?

Due to the heavy despair felt as the place to go down has been lost
With the empty heart filled with tears
The body collapsed at the roadside

The vacant steps
Go along time and
The fall onto empty fallen leaves is lonely

# 덧없는 길

가을은 바람이 되었습니다
나무에게 와서 붉은 옷을 입혔습니다
하늘은 샘이 나서 바다에 풍덩 빠졌습니다

가을은 혼자 점점 고독하였습니다
달에게 다가가서 외로움을 전했습니다
달빛은 하염없이 차가운 빛만 냅니다

아무것도 모르는 별들은
서로 옹기종기 모여서 밤새껏 이야기하는데
어느덧 동녘은 여명을 안고 기지개합니다.

모두가 뿔뿔이 사라졌습니다.

# Transient Way

The fall has become a wind
And came to the trees to clothe them in red.
The sky became jealous and jumped into the sea.

The fall has become increasingly lonely
And thus went to the moon to let the moon know loneliness
The moon just vacantly emits cold light

Knowing nothing, stars
Are huddled and talk through the night
Before we know, the east embraces dawn and stretches itself.

Everyone disperses and disappears

# 의심의 돌

달콤한 말을 작은 시심詩心에 심어
그대 앞에 바치던
그때

한숨은 그리움의 골짜기에 살았고
함께 있고 싶은 마음은
처녀림 속에 흐르는 시냇물이었는데

지금은
메말라버린 감동의 끝자락에 서서
픽션의 돌을 줍는다

물수제비뜨는 돌은
서러운 파문破紋만 남기고
고통의 물속에 빠진다

어쩔 수 없는 구름 한 조각
물 위에 떠 돌다
바람에 밀려 정처 없이 서러움에 떤다

# Stone of Suspicion

At that time
When I planted sweet words in a poetic turn of mind
And gave you

Sighs lived in the valley of longing
And the mind wanting to be with you
A brook flowing through a virgin forest

Now
Standing at the end of dried sensation
I pick up stones of faction

Stones used to play ducks and drakes
Just leave sad ripples
And drown in the water of pain

Not knowing what to do, a piece of cloud
Floats on the water
And pushed by winds to wander about trembling with sorrow

# 애환哀歡의 길목에서

쉴 곳 찾아 헤매다
낯선 골목에서
당신을 보았습니다

구부러진 골목은
애환과 정겨움이 땀 냄새와 어울려
삶의 옷깃을 적시고 있습니다

곧은길에 익숙한 세월
나의 영혼의 눈이 멀어
당신을 보지 못할까 걱정입니다.

내 앞에 펼쳐진 골목 길
세상의 깊이와 넓이를 느끼며
당신 앞에 무거운 짐을 내려놓습니다.

# At a Street Corner of Joys and Sorrows

In search for a place of rest,
in an unfamiliar alley,
I saw you.

In the bending alleys
sadness, happiness and affection mixes with the smell of sweat
and soaks the collars of life.

The days spend on straight paths,
I am worried that the eyes of my soul goes blind
and that I might not be able to see you.

The alley in front of me,
feeling the depth and width of the world,
I rest my heavy burdens in front of you.

# 퇴색

가을은 바람이 되었습니다
나무에게 붉은 옷을 입혔습니다
하늘은 파랗게 질렸습니다.

빛 잃은 낮달은
어둠의 바다에 풍덩 빠졌습니다
물결은 하얗게 조각났습니다

아무것도 모르는 별들은
옹기종기 밤새껏 속삭이는데
어느덧 동녘은 여명을 안고 기지개합니다.

채색된 잎은 낙엽으로
모두가 뿔뿔이 사라졌습니다.
가을은 혼자 점점 외로워 갔습니다

# Fading

Autumn has become winds
It clothes the trees in red
The sky has been frightened blue.

The day moon that has lost its light
Falls into the sea of darkness
Waves were broken into white pieces

Knowing nothing, stars
Are huddled and talk through the night
The east embraces dawn and stretches itself.

Colored leaves as fallen leaves
All disappear separately
Fall has become increasingly lonely

# 질투심嫉妬心

있지도 않은 일을
픽션으로 쓰려는 마음
지나친 사랑의 표출일까

믿음은 질투를 허물지만
의심은 자신을 곪게 하는데
왜 하필 삼류소설을 써야 하나

대금 소리는 빈속에서 나오지만
불에 닿으면 마디 터지는 소리
입술은 피곤타

순풍은 씨앗을 높이 날게 하나
강풍은 잎을 꺾이게 하는데
마음엔 끊임없이 갈등의 비가 내린다

# Jealousy

Things that did not happen
The mind trying to write fiction
Is it an expression of excessive love?

Though trust tears jealousy down
Suspicion matures
Why should he write a dime novel of all things

Though the sound of a Daigeum comes from its hollow inside
The sounds of bursting joints when it has come into contact with fire
The lips are tired

Though fair winds make seeds fly high
Strong winds bend the leaves
In my mind, the rain of conflict comes unceasingly

# 부메랑

붉게 물든 저녁놀 뒤에
적막한 밤이 보인다

몇 분 후 지구가 멸망한다면
무엇을 할까
아무도 결정을 못 하련만

시간의 마디마다 맺힌 한恨을
용서容恕로 풀고 파도
남아 있는 호흡이 모자란다

슬픔도 기쁨도 잠재우는
어두움일지라도
한 걸음 더 나가 축복하고 싶다

사람은 바람의 옷을 빌려 입었지만
삶의 모자는 부메랑인 것을…….

# Boomerang

At the rear of the evening glow dyed red
A silent night is seen

If the earth should come to an end
What shall we do
Nobody should be able to decide

Though I want to vent the spites formed at each knot of time
With forgiveness
My remaining breaths are insufficient

Even if it is the darkness that
Puts sorrows and joys into sleep
I would like to take a step forward and bless

Though humans have borrowed and are wearing the clothes of the wind
The hat of life is a boomerang…….

# 노을에 피는 시심詩心

허공에 한해가 바쁘게 흐르는데
함께 달음박질하는
기억이 숨차다

바람의 입술이 파리해지고
시간에 매달린 잎들조차
붙들 수 있는 힘이 소진消盡된다

나는 작은 마음 위에
현실의 펜으로
망각의 글을 쓴다

희미한 흔적들이
또박또박 되살아나
이름 모를 나라의 성城을 쌓는다

# A Poetic Turn of Mind that Blooms at the Glow of the Setting Sun

A year flows in a hurry in the void
Running together with it
The memory is short of breath

The lips of the wind become pale
And even the power to hold the leaves hanging on time
Is exhausted

With a small mind
and a pen of reality
I write a writing of forgetting

Vague traces
Clearly revive
To build a castle in a country of an unknown name

# 찻잔

작은 찻잔 속에 담은
눈물 한 방울

다시는 못 갈
추억의 뒤안길

이제 와서 돌아보면
소용없어도

소중히 간직하는
삶의 그림자

깊은 밤
몸서리치는 나의 넋두리

찻잔 속 봄은
이렇게 외로운가 보다

# A Teacup

A teardrop
Placed in a small teacup

Back roads of memory
That cannot be untrod

When thinking about now
Although it is useless

There is a shadow of life
Kept preciously

In the night
My shuddering grumbles

I guess the Spring of a teacup
Is lonely like this

# 귀의歸依

메마른 땅이
나의 뿌리조차 시들게 하여
영혼조차 썩게 하는데
개미지옥과 같은 벌레가
싹을 자른다.

애닯게 울어도 봐줄 이 없고
외면의 눈초리에 식은땀 흘리는
자궁에 갇혀버린 유산될 배아가 된다

시간이 흘러도 무너지지 않는
고통
혈관 속에 혈액마저 굳어버려
심장은 분노로 싸늘하다

나오기 싫은 문을 열고
나올 수밖에 없는 운명도 기구하다.
저주가 입술에서 자라고
이글거리는 분노의 파고가 높다

# Conversion

Dried up land
Drys up my roots
And rots my soul
Bugs like ant-lions
Cut up the roots

No matter how sad the cry, there is nobody to look
The embryo, trapped inside a womb, will be aborted
Sweating cold sweat from neglectful looks

Pain that does not break down with the passage of time
Hardens the blood in its veins
And chills the heart with its rage

The destiny rejected
Through an unwilling door
With curses on its lips
The boiling rage has high waves

하늘에 구멍이 뚫렸다.
빛이다. 현란한 빛 그 자체다
육신을 태우고
분노를 태우는데 충분히 뜨겁다.
활활 태워라
볼록렌즈의 초점이 그곳에 머물러
그 더러운 재조차 남기지 말고
다 태워버려라
사랑은 빛보다 위대하나니…….

A hole in the sky
A bright hostile light
Hot enough to burn the flesh
And the rage
Hovers in the focus of a convex lens
To burn everything
Without leaving dirty ash behind
Love is greater than that light

# 기차여행

걸어와도 아쉽고
타고와도 아쉬운
여정의 길

허느적 거리는 허수아비처럼
바람 따라 구름 따라 밀려왔건만
남은 건 후회뿐

끝없이 뻗쳐있는 레일 위에서
영 · 육의 두 바퀴로 달리고 있는
세월이 요란하게 지나가는데
세워야 할 정류장이 보이질 않는다.

내려놓고 가야 할 짐이 많은데
서러움도 괴로움도
사랑조차 내려놓고
가야할 이 길

종착역에 기다리는
그이 앞에서

# Train Trip

The path of a trip
Which is sad to walk
Which is sad to ride

Although drawn by the wind and clouds
Like a boneless scarecrow
Only regret remains

The time passes loudly
On an endlessly stretched rail
With two wheels of soul and flesh
And no visible places to rest

There are many burdens;
Sorrows, pains, and love;
to be put down,
on this rail

Without regrets or shame
And with delightful smiles

아쉬움도 부끄럼도 가지지 않고
환희의 미소로 만나고 싶다

It would be grand to meet
The one waiting at the station

# 광대

신은 인간에게 춤의 옷을 입히고
노래의 영혼을 주었으니
비록 옷이 세월에 찢겨져
바람에 흩날려도
영혼을 위하여
노래하며 춤을 추자

기쁨과 슬픔도 손을 잡고
운명아 춤을 춰라
광대가 되어

테이레시아스의 저주여 함께 춤을 춰라
남자가 되든 여자가 되든
주관자가 있으리니
운명의 게놈은 이미 정해져 있는 것

# Clown

God put a dancing garment on man
And gave him a singing soul
So even with garments torn by time
Or fluttering in the wind
Let's sing and dance
For our souls

By holding hands with joy and sorrow
Destiny! Become a clown
And Dance

Teiresias's curse! Dance together
The destiny of the genome
Is predetermined by the Administrator
Whether to be a boy or a girl

장차 무엇이 되어
어디로 갈지 모르는 인생아
질투의 화염 속에서
사랑하는 이와 함께
비 오는 거리나 바람 부는 언덕에서
이글거리는 속내를 꾹꾹 눌러가며
지치도록 춤을 추자
세월 따라가다가 모래알처럼 허물어져
춤이 멈추어질 때까지

Doesn't know which direction the life will go
Nor become what in the future
In the flame of jealousy
Let's dance until exhaustion
With a lover
On a rainy street or a windy hill
Suppressing glaring minds
Until the dancing stops
Ground down like sand in the passage of time

# 변심變心

계절마다 바꿔 입는 옷에 길들여진 탓일까
뭐든지 바꿔야 하는 직성直星이라면
차라리 그리워하지나 말 것을

너만 사랑한다는 말
쓸데없이 뇌까리는 죽음의 비산砒酸으로
쉬이 탈바꿈하는 언어

세상을 주고도 못 바꿀
너란
휴지에 쓰는 불신의 낙서가 된 것을

삶의 디지털 메모리에서
삭제될 육신은
영원의 문에서 좌절해 버린 그리움뿐

점화點火가 잘 되는 나무일수록
쉬이 검은 숯으로 타 버릴 속
드디어 하얀 재災로 흩어지고 말 것을…….

# A Change of Heart

If the habit of changing clothes each season
Breeds satisfaction through continuous change
Then how is it that I miss you

'You are the only one I love'
Is just words; easily changed
With the arsenic of uselessly repeating death

More precious than the world,
Yet, you are
Reduced to unreliable scribbles on a tissue

Flesh destined for deletion
From the digital memory of life
Leaves residue of frustrated regret at the door to the eternity

Trees that can easily lit
Inside can be easily carbonized
And finally scattered as white ash

# 닫힌 대화對話

꽃을 심고 가꾸자고
울타리를 만들었다
세월을 한 움큼 비료처럼 뿌렸다

줄기에 언어로 긁어버린 상처로
작은 꽃봉오리 맺기가
어려운 걸까?

생기 잃은 꽃봉오리
피지를 못해
서러움에 노랗다

예쁜 꽃 피지 않아도
진종일 서성이던 정원에서
상처傷處만 더듬는다.

# Closed Conversation

A wooden fence
Surrounds a flower garden
Fertilized with a handful of time

How much effort
To sprout little buds
With stems scarred by harsh words?

Drained of vitality
Buds yellowed by sadness
Stunted; infertile

In the blossomless plot
Fumbled and scarred
The gardener putters each day

# 노숙자

하늘을 바라보며 사랑을 했고
지평선을 바라보며 뛰었던 시간들

계획된 행복한 여행은
강한 분노에 조각나고
가까운 장래에 정상으로 올라
세상을 보려던 꿈은
물거품으로 사라진다.

잃어버린 사랑에
가슴은 허기져
더 빼앗길 것 없는데도
내 마음은 차가운 지하도 계단에
잔뜩 웅크리고 앉아 있다.

동정의 눈들은
가식의 안경을 끼고
바이러스로 이룬 몸 덩인 양
멀리서 던져 넣는 몇 푼의 동정심에
자선가처럼 지나가는 가상의 영상影像들.
보는 눈이 더 슬프다

# Homeless

I stared at the sky and fell in love
I stared at the horizon and ran

Planned pleasure trips
Shattered to pieces by furious anger
And the dream to look down at the world
By climbing to the top
Disappears in bubbles

For lost love
My heart is starved
Although there is no more to lose
My mind is curled up
On the stairs of a cold underpass

Pitying eyes
With fake eyeglasses
A few coins of pity thrown from far away
As if they are made of viruses
Fake images passing by like men of charity
Watching them makes me feel more sad

텅 비운 마음에
찬바람 먼저 알고 들어와
줄곧 혈관을 흐르는 뜨겁던 의욕을
차디찬 콘크리트 바닥에 엎드려
구걸케 한다.

아직 나는
내 영혼과 더불어
따뜻한 집에서 머물고 있는데…….

In an emptied mind
Cold wind knew and entered
Made me beg
For the hot desire that flew in my blood vein
By laying on the ice-cold concrete floor

Yet I stay
In a warm house
With my soul together……

# 별

안개에 너의 얼굴이 묻혔어도
바람에 자태가 실려 가도
풀잎 끝에 맺힌 영롱한 이슬에
빛으로 사라진 그림자를 찾는다.

광활한 들에 자라는 풀잎에
외로운 산길에 서성이는 잎새에
나무가 우거진 갈등葛藤의 덩굴에도

눈물로 방울져야 할
운명이기에
이토록 가슴이 시려 오는구나.

잎이 떨어져도 눈물이 되지 말고
나무가 흔들려도 겁내지 말고
행여, 꿈에라도 내 가슴에 내릴지니

그리운 모습 지울 수 없어
너의 영혼만이라도 별이 되어
내가 쳐다볼 때만 반짝일지라.

# Star

Although your face is covered by fog
Although you are carried by the wind
Look for the shadow that disappears in light
From bright dew formed on the end of a leaf

On the grass covering a vast field
On leaves hovering on a lonely mountain path
In bushes of conflict overgrown with trees

It is your destiny
To form as tears
Which makes my heart so cold

Don't become tears even if the leaves fall
Don't be scared even if the trees sway
By chance, you may fall into my heart in a dream

Can not erase you from longing
Become a star at least with your soul
And twinkle only when I look

# 시간의 망루에 서서

네 눈빛 속
감춰진 깊은 사랑 느끼지만
망설이는 발걸음이 몹시 무겁다.

달려온 긴 하루가 어느새 저물고
별이 내리는 들판을 함께 가려 해도
시간이 먼저 나의 등을 떠미는구나

닫히는 시간의 문
기다릴 수 없어
혼자서 울먹이며 밤길을 간다.

밤이 끝나는 곳 다다라서
별이 되어 너를 지키리니
두려움 없이 밤길을 걸어오려무나.

우리 서로 만나, 그리움을 수놓은 별이 되어
연인戀人들의 가슴에
환희의 별빛으로 내리자꾸나

## Standing at the Lookover of Time

In your eyes
Is a deep hidden love
But hesitant steps are heavy

The long busy day grew dark
Trying to take the field together where stars shoot
But time presses ever onward

The closing door of time
Cannot wait
So I walk on a dark road sobbing alone

At the place where the night ends
I will become your guardian star
So come walk on the night road without fear

Let's meet and become stars that embroider longing
And shoot into lovers' hearts
Star filled with the light of joy

# 포도

햇볕은 구름을 달구어
지표에서 이어 온 인연因緣의 넝쿨에
그리움을 단다.

한여름은 잎 사이를 지나며
초록빛 바람을 끌어다 정념情念을 식히고
보랏빛 성숙으로 물들게 한다.

이제, 옷을 벗고
당신 곁으로 다가가
오랜 인고의 옷고름을 풀어헤쳐

한 알 한 알 품고 있는
못다 한 사랑을 잔盞속에 녹여
혈관을 데우련다.

환희의 파도가 높게 일어
육체가 포말로 사라져도
이 밤을 당신과 함께 지새우고 싶다

# Grapes

The sunlight heats up the clouds
And hangs longing
On a bush of connection made in the earth

Summer passes through leaves
Brings green wind to cool down passion
And dyes with purple maturity

Now, take off the clothing
Draw closer together
Remove the coverings of long patience

Burn the blood vessels
Melt each unrealized grain of love
In a tea cup

Even the body will disappear in bubbles
With high waves of pleasure
I would like to stay with you this night

# 가까이 더 가까이

당신을 생각하는 고요한 이 시간
산 위에 운행하는 신비한 구름 속에
감춰 논 내 마음
하나씩 꺼내어 보여드리리니
이해가 어려워
발걸음이 무거워도
나에게 오셔요.

산 아래 살아도 하늘을 봐요.
대중은 구경꾼
그 속에 그대 서 있지 말고
가까이 더 가까이 곁으로 오셔요

원망
불평
교만으로 물들어 가는
산 아래 사는 인생이지만

## Closer and Closer

In this quiet time thinking about you
I will show you my heart
Hidden in a mysterious cloud
Passing above a mountain
Although it is difficult to understand
And your footsteps are heavy
Please come to me

Even if living under a mountain, see the sky
The public is just bystanders
Don't just stand there
Come closer and closer

Although life is dyed with
Resentment
Complaints
And arrogance under a mountain

옷자락을 만져 나은 혈우병 여인처럼
값진 믿음 가지고
가까이 더 가까이 다가오셔요
살아가는 이유가 무엇이든 간에
모든 정성 다 하여
그대 품으리라

Like the woman who was healed by touching the hem of His garment
With the valuable belief
Come closer and closer
Whatever the reason for living
I will embrace you
With all my effort

# 상흔傷痕

강을 건너려 걷어 올린 옷자락
젖을수록 깊은 강물
온몸을 적신다

나를 훑고 지나가는 물은
짜릿한 전율戰慄을 느끼는
격정激情의 환호성歡呼聲

젖은 옷을 위선僞善에 말리는
초췌憔悴한 양심
변명辨明으로 어눌한 입술이 부끄럽다

강물은 지평선 넘어 흐르는데
갈대밭 사이를 말없이 지나는
하얀 낮달이 부럽다

# Scars

Hems tucked up to cross
A river that gets deeper as
It wets the whole body

The water that passes through me
Is the exclamation of passion
Giving a thrilling tremble

Haggard conscience
Drying wet clothing on hypocrisy
Inarticulate lips make shameful excuses

The river flows over the horizon
Envious of the white daytime moon
Passing the fields of reeds without a word

# 아득한 그리움

풀잎에 맺힌 이슬
그리움이 스며들어 영롱히 빛나는데

기다리다 지쳐
눈시울에 맺힌 이슬 별빛 머금어
검은 하늘 속으로 굴러서 간다.

그리워하다 마는 인생
저승까지 눈물만 굴러갈 건가?

# Distant Longing

Dew formed on grass leaf
Sparkling brightly; infiltrated with longing

Tired of waiting
Dew formed on eyes filled with starlight
Rolls into the dark sky

If a life ends from only longing
Do the tears roll all the way to hell?

# 괴로운 일

잊으려면
자꾸 생각나는 것은
그대의 언어

괴롭거나 외로울 때
위로慰勞 되었던
'사랑한다' 한마디 말

오히려 그 말을 잊어야 하는
그토록 괴로운 일
어디 있을까

# Painful Thing

When trying to forget
I keep remembering
The way you speak

When I am stressed or lonely
The comforting words
'I Love You'

How sad it is
That I have to
Forget about those words

# 그곳에

활활 타오르다
다 태우지 못하고 밤이 다가왔다
소진消盡될 삶이 그리움인 줄 모르고
마냥 너만 그리워했다

타다 남은 빛이
어둠을 밀어낼 줄 알았는데
짙은 고독만 그리움을 삼킨다.

언젠가 안개가 자욱한 깊은 산 속
우리가 만났던 그곳이
아직 내 마음에 머무는 것은
그대 잊지 못하기 때문이라

끝없이 외로움을 태우는 노을로
아니면 다시 흩어질 안개라도 좋으니
그곳에 잠시 머물러
꺼져가는 불씨를 마저 태우고 싶다

# Over There

Blazed up
But the night came before it burned off
Did not know if the life that will be exhausted is a longing itself
And just missed you

Thought that the leftover light from burning
Would push the darkness out
But the thick loneliness swallowed the longing

The place where we met
In a foggy deep forest
Stays in my mind
Because I cannot forget about you

Like the sunset burns the loneliness endlessly
Or like a fog that will be scattered anyway
I would like to stay there for a moment
To burn the dying ember

어둠이 빛을 품어 별을 출산하면
별빛을 모아
그곳에 내려 우리 서로 만나
계곡에서 피어나는 안개로 그리움을 덮으리라

When the darkness gives birth to stars
By collecting starlight
We will meet over there
And cover the longing with fog rising from the valley

# 열병熱病

괜찮다고 해놓고
소식이 늦어도
조금만 멀리 가도
불안한 마음

믿으면서
믿기지 않는
묘妙한 생각

할 말은 많은데
만나면 말 못하고
헤어지면 아쉬운
고뇌苦惱의 갈증渴症

# Fever

Everything seemed to be ok
But feelings of insecurity creep in
When the news comes late
When went a little far

Trust
But doesn't trust
Which are odd thoughts

There are many things to say
That will not come out when we meet
Separation causes such sadness
And the thirst of anguish

# 당신이 있기에

깜깜한 하늘에 별이 없다면
당신을 쳐다보지 못하고
하늘에 흐르는 달이 없다면
당신을 기다릴 수 없을 겁니다.

별은 보이는데
아무리 애써도 보이지 않는
당신의 얼굴

언제면 오실 건가요?
언제쯤 내 손을 잡아주실 건가요?
당신을 사랑하기에 고독합니다.

고통이 싫지만 성숙하게 되고
고독을 통하여야만
당신을 보게 되는가 봅니다

목이 갈渴해도 물보라같이 시원한 것은
당신의 음성 때문이며
내 손이 비었어도 행복한 것은
당신이 있기 때문입니다.

# Because You Exist

If there were no stars in the dark sky
I might not look at you
If there was no moon flowing in the sky
I might not wait for you

I see the stars
But no matter what I do,
I can't see your face

When will you come?
When will you hold my hand?
I feel lonely because I love you

Although I don't like pain, I have matured
I guess that I can only see you
Through the loneliness

Because of your voice
I felt a cool mist in spite of my thirst
And because you exist
I am happy in spite of my empty hands

# 슬픈 정원

당신이 없어도 그리운 것은
내 마음에 함께 가꾼
정원이 있기 때문입니다

허물어진 울타리 아래
당신의 눈물이 떨어진 자리에는
안개꽃이 슬프게 피어납니다.

지나가던 바람도 잠시 머물러
애처롭게 어루만지며
흐느낍니다.

흔적조차 없어질 정원 위를
하얀 쪽배 구름은
눈물 몇 방울 떨구며 흘러갑니다.

# Garden of Sorrow

I miss you when you are not here
Because of the garden
That you made in my mind

In the places where your tears fell
Under the broken fence
Gypsophila grows in sorrow

The passing wind stops for a moment
Then, sobs
Patting with pity

Above a disappearing garden
A white floating cloud
Flows by and drops a few tears

# 작은 소원所願

배는 항구에
머물러 있기 위해서 있는 것이 아니라
파도를 헤치며 항해를 하기 위함이라

사랑하며 괴로워함도
이별하기 위함이 아니라
높은 질고의 삶을 헤쳐나기 위함이니

어이,
듣고 싶은 좋은 말만 들어야 하고
삶의 황홀함만 보아야 할 것인가

어깨가 으스러지고
발이 아파 걸을 수 없어도
손을 잡고 부축副軸하며 걸어야 하리니

내 사랑하는 자여, 후일後日
낙원樂園에 배가 정박碇泊할 때까지
인내忍耐로써 파고波高를 넘어야 해요.

# A Small Wish

A ship
Is meant to plow through the waves
Not to just stay still

Loving and suffering
Is meant to plow through the painful life
Not to be separated

Hey,
Desire to hear only the sweet words
Seek out the ecstasy of the life

Even if shoulders are crushed
Unable to walk from foot pain
Walk by holding hands and helping each other

Someday, my dear,
Let's go over the waves with patience
Until the ship come to anchor in heaven

# 태화강

네온사인에 현란하게 흔들리는
태화강
보름달이 오히려 초췌하다

하얗게 지친 달은
태화교 위를 오가는 차들을
물끄러미 바라본다.

고요한 바다에 자맥질하던 달이
은파 되어 별들과 놀던
그리운 옛 강변

지나던 구름이 안쓰러워
세월에 씻긴 보름달을 가리는데
왠지 하늘조차 슬프다

# Tae Hwa River

Tae Hwa River
With flashy waving from neon signs
Makes the full moon look lonely

The exhausted pale moon
Stares at vehicles
Crossing the Tae Hwa Bridge

Bring back the old riverside
Where the moon dove into the silent sea
And played with the stars on silvery moonlit waves

A passing cloud feels pity
And hides the time-faded full moon
And somehow even the sky feels sorrow

# 어느 선거選擧

노욕老慾은 춤춘다
갖은 감언이설로 표를 모았다
모여든 마음 밭에 뿌려야 할 씨앗은
믿음인데
우리圈牢를 만들어 문턱엔
무지의 쇠고랑 찬 총채벌레만 모았다

맑은 공기에
푸른 하늘만 이고 살았던 고추는
대체할 약이 없다

총채벌레가 퍼트리는 바이러스에
고춧잎이 아무리 고함쳐도
목청이 없다

침탈로 찢겨진 상처
짓눌린 꽃망울 피우려
한없이 울었으나 눈물이 없다

## An Election

The elderly danced around greedily
Collecting votes with eloquence
Spreading seeds over the collective mind fields Of what should be trust
But only the Thysanoptera, with cuffs of stupidity, are gathered on the doorsill of a pen

There is no alternative medicine for
Peppers carried by the blue sky
With clean air

No matter how the pepper leaves roar out
They have no voice
Against the virus spread by the Thysanoptera

The scars left by invasions
Cried out endlessly
For the oppressed bud to bloom

꽃을 피웠다
하얄 뿐이다
독기처럼 스민 창백한 분노

마음의 분노로
고추는 익는다.

The flower that bloomed
A blossom of pure white
Permeated by the poison of pale resentment

Pepper ripens
In the light of resentment

# TV 드라마

TV 속이 썩었는지 드라마가 온통 제정신이 아니다.
예쁜 인형들은 각본의 글줄 따라
전부 탈선한다.

탈선의 경마장은 진흙투성이다
도덕과 윤리는 흰개미의 침입으로
썩어버린 통나무
어디까지 썩어야 할지 모른다

세대와 세대로 이어가는 고통이
언제 멈출지 모르는 형벌일까?

아침이나 저녁이나 TV 보는 날은
간이나 심장이 있는지 쓰다듬어야 할 시간
부모의 근심된 마음만 출렁일 뿐

TV의 창마다 검은색을 칠할 수 없고
썩어 문드러질 모습만 눈으로 들어온다.
다시는 안 봐야지 하면서도 또 보게 되는
중독된 머리여!

# TV Drama

Perhaps the TV is rotten, but dramas are out of their minds.
Pretty dolls follow the script
and all become erratic.

The race track of deviation is filled with mud.
Morals and ethics are attacked by mites,
and a rotten piece of wood.
Nobody knows to where it will rot.

Pains that are passed down from one generation to the next,
is it punishment that nobody knows when it will stop?

When watching TV in the morning or evening
That's the time to pat the liver or heart
Only the parents' mind sloshes

But can't color the TV screens black
Eyes pulled to figures that will soon rot away
In spite of efforts not to watch
And yet, here I sit watching
Addicted in spite of myself!

# 망상妄想

허망하게 걸어온 세월
되돌아갈 수 없어
모두가 한숨 되어 창가에 서리구나

창밖에는 새싹 파릇한데
어인 일로 자욱한 안개에
스며오는 어두움 뿐

햇빛이 강하면 그림자도 강한데
나는
육신과 그림자가 따로 노는구나

그림자가 나를 떠날 때
한 줌의 재가 될지
흙이 될지 모르지만

그때엔
기쁨도 슬픔도
허망할 마음조차 있을 수 없어라

# Delusion

Times passed in vain,
I cannot return to
and turns into sighs and fogs up the window.

Out of the window new shoots are green,
but for some reason thick fogs,
and a darkness that spreads.

When the sun is strong so is its shadow,
and I
have a different body and shadow.

When my shadow leaves me
it may become a handful of ash
or perhaps even dirt.

At that time,
no happiness and no sadness,
not even a heart to have remorse for will be left.

# 좌훈

썩어버릴 육체의 갈망이 지나가면
파산을 시킬 무서운 파도가 다가와
삶의 항해를 괴롭혀도
따뜻한 사랑의 입김이 서려오는 아궁이 속에서
잠시 쉬어본다

옛 조상들이 두고 간 아궁이 속으로
나의 영혼이 빠져들면
서러운 정, 고운 정이 무엇인지를
가만히 귓속에 전하여 온다.

따뜻한 온기가 스며오면
온 전신에 혈액이 감돈다
사랑이 흐른다

마디마디 스며있는 고통은 사라지고
뿌리에서 빨아올린 삶의 정념이 잎들에 전달될 때
줄기에는 꽃을 피우고
열매 맺을 준비에 자궁이 꿈틀댄다.

## Hip Fumigation

When the desires of the body that will rot away pass,
a terrifying wave that will bring bankruptcy comes.
Even if it disturbs the navigation of life,
in the furnace that steams up breaths of warm love,
I rest for a minute.

When into the furnace that our ancestors left us,
my soul dives in,
what sad and kind-hearted affection is,
it gently comes into my ear.

When warmth seeps in,
blood circulates throughout the body,
and love flows.

Pain in each joint vanishes
and when the passion of life brought up from the roots arrive at the leaves,
flowers on the stems blossom,
and the uterus trembles in preparation to bring fruit.

사랑의 밀어를 품은 좌훈의 연기는
하늘에 있는 별을 향해
끊임없이 흐르고 또 흐른다.

The steam of the hip fumigator that holds the whispers of love
ceaselessly flows and flows again
to the stars in the heaven.

| 서평 |

# 생의 열정과 기다림

변종환

| Critique |

# Passion and Waiting of Life

Jong Hwan Byeon

| 서평 |

# 생의 열정과 기다림

변종환
( 시인 · 부산광역시문인협회 회장 )

"나는 홀로 있었다. 나는 기다리고 있었고 나의 모든 작품들도 또한 기다리고 있었다. 어느 날, 나는 발레리를 읽었다. 그리고 나의 기다림이 끝났다는 것을 알았다."

시인 릴케는 이처럼 절감하는 감동적인 말을 남겼다. 이 말이 겸허한 것은 물론이고 눈을 뜨고 깨어있는 자는 누구나 알아들을 말이다.

"기다리고 있었"던 것은 비단 릴케만이 아니었을 것이다. 수많은 사람들이 수많은 시간 동안 기다리고 있었던 것이다. 이토록 우리의 기다림의 빈 공간을 결정적으로 채워줄 그 무엇이 남아 있을까.

| Critique |

# Passion and Waiting of Life

Jong Hwan Byeon

(Poet / Chairperson of the Busan Writers' Association)

"I was alone. I waited and ally my works also waited. One day, I read Valery. And I knew that my wait was over."

This emotional passage was written by the poet, Rilke. Anyone who is humble and are awake with their eyes open can understand what this means.

"Rilke was not the only one who was 'waiting'. Many people were waiting for very long times. So what is left to fill the empty space of our waiting once and for all?

We are always asked the question, 'why do you write poems and work on literature?'

'왜 시를 쓰고 문학을 하는가?' 라는 물음은 항상 우리를 따라다닌다.

왜 시를 쓰는가 하는 질문은 너는 왜 밥을 먹지 않고 빵을 먹느냐 하는 질문과 동일하다. 시를 쓰는 사람은 음악을 듣는 사람보다 조금 더 시에 대한 관심을 가지고 있을 뿐이지 음악을 전혀 듣지 않는 것은 아니다. 악기를 연주하는 사람은 음악에 대한 관심도가 시를 쓰는 행위보다 더 높을 따름이지 시에 전혀 관심이 없다는 것은 아니다.

시를 쓴다는 것은 가치 있는 것을 기록하는 것이며 아름답기 위하여 시를 쓴다고 할 수 있다. 그러나 진정한 아름다움을 알기 위해서는 추한 뒷모습을 보는 눈이 필요하다.

결국, 우리는 아름답기 위하여 시를 쓰고 진정한 아름다움을 알기 위해서는 추한 뒷모습을 보는 눈이 필요하다. 시를 향한 끝없는 접근은 무한히 먼 거리에서부터 무한히 먼 거리에 있는 소실점을 향해 나아가는 도정道程이며 감미로운 작업이다. 오늘도 시를 읽고 시를 사는 삶의 방식은 아름답다. 한 편의 시를 노래하고 착한 사람들과 멋진 자연환경과 이웃하며 살아간다는 것은 생명의 환희이다.

이명희 시인은 생활 현장에서 시를 섭렵하는 시인이

The question why we write poems is the same as if I asked why do you eat? People who write poems simply have more interest in poems compared to those who listen to music, but it does not mean that they do not listen to music at all. People who play instruments are just more interested in music than poetry, but it does not mean that they are completely uninterested in poems.

Writing poems is the act of recording what is valuable to us and we write poetry to make such records more beautiful. But in order to know what true beauty is, we must have the ability to see the ugly, dark side as well.

In result, we write poetry to become beautiful and we must have an eye for the ugly, dark side to know true beauty. The endless approach to poetry is a path heading towards a vanishing point from a very far place to an infinitely further place, and it is a sweet and mellow work. Even today, the way of reading poetry and living poetry is beautiful. Singing poems and being neighbors to nice people and the beautiful natural environment is the joy of life.

Poet Myung Hee Lee is a poet who is well read in poems in everyday life. She joined the literary world with a new poet award in the Busan Society of Poets 'Busan Poets'. She is currently the CEO of Comely.

다. 부산시인협회 계간 『부산시인』 신인상으로 문단에 나온 그는 (주)캄리의 CEO이다.

이번에 탄생하는 이명희 시인의 첫 시집 『이브여, 눈을 뜨라』는 모두 마흔아홉 편의 시로 채워져 있다.

이 시집 서문에서도 밝혔듯이 그는 “아무리 바빠도 우리의 생활 속에서 아름답고 보람 있는 생활을 추구하기 위하여 시간이 있을 때마다 조금씩 조금씩 나의 마음을 모아둔 것을 시집으로 내게 된 것”이라고 자신의 문학적 소회를 말하고 있다. 오늘 우리의 사회 환경은 여성들의 사회진출이 괄목할 만하다. 각계각층에 포진되어 있는 여성의 수는 급증했으며 그 역할도 크게 늘어났다. 이명희 시인의 첫 시집 제명題名을 『이브여, 눈을 뜨라』고 한 것도 이러한 시대적 소명을 암시하는 것으로 생각된다.

먼저 이 시집의 표제시 「이브여, 눈을 뜨라」는 시인 특유의 감성으로 시적 대상을 형상화시켜나가고 있다.

잠들어 꿈꾸기조차 어려워
우리는 주어진 틀 속에서 살았고
신음은 어두운 밤하늘에서 떠날 줄 몰랐다

차가운 옷을 벗고
속박에서 벗어나는 새싹들
저기, 몸을 녹일 훈훈한 바람이 있구나

벌써 봄은 지나고 여름인데
욕망의 굴레를 어느 전쟁터에서 얻은 전리품처럼

Myung Hee Lee's first collection of poems, 'Eve, Open Your Eyes', is comprised of a total of nine poems.

As stated in the preface of her book, she explains her impressions of literature saying, "to publish this book of poems that I gathered bit by bit whenever I had the luxury to in order to pursue a beautiful and fulfilling life no matter how busy life becomes." In today's society, women are very active in society. The number of women taking part in different parts of society and life has risen exponentially and their roles have become much more important as well. I believe that the reason why poet Myung Hee Lee titled her collection of poems 'Eve, Open Your Eyes' is in light of such.

First, her title poem 'Eve, Open Your Eyes', visually describes what she sees with her unique sentiment.

> Too hard to dream while sleeping
> we live in a frame given unto us,
> and moans know not how to leave the dark night sky.
>
> Taking off their cold clothes,
> shoots emerge from their shackles,
> and there, warm wind to melt the body comes.
>
> Spring has passed and it is summer,
> but the restraints of desires are like spoils of war,

허리에 동여매고 살아야 하는 조작된 행복

이제,
바람이 치마를 펄럭이게 하고
뜨거운 태양은 그대들의 옷을 벗게 하나니
이브여, 눈을 뜨라

다가오는 가을에 결실을 위해
환희여 빛깔로 아끼고, 사랑하자
이브여, 눈을 뜨라

-「이브여, 눈을 뜨라」 전문

"잠들어 꿈꾸기조차 어려워/우리는 주어진 틀 속에서 살았고/신음은 어두운 밤하늘에서 떠날 줄 몰랐"다는 첫 연의 진술은 시인이 서문에서 밝힌 것처럼 수년 동안 어려움을 극복하고 일터를 구축한 삶의 진솔한 마음을 엿볼 수 있게 한다.

이 시 4연에서는 "이제/바람이 치마를 펄럭이게 하고/뜨거운 태양은 그대들의 옷을 벗게 하나니/이브여, 눈을 뜨"라고 다짐하는 시인은 "다가오는 가을에 결실을 위해"서 모든 것을 아끼고 사랑하자고 그 이유를 말한다.

시인의 임무, 어쩌면 유일한 임무는 아마도 시를 준비하고 다듬는 일일 것이다. 시인은 시를 창조하기보다는 시를 영접한다는 말이 더 적합하지 않을까 싶다. 시인은

which are tied around our waists as fabricated happiness.

Now,
the wind flaps the skirt,
and the hot sun undresses you, so
Eve, open your eyes.

For the fruits of the coming autumn,
joy, save your colors and love,
Eve, open your eyes.

- 'Eve, Open Your Eyes'

The first paragraph "Too hard to dream while sleeping / we live in a frame given unto us, / and moans know not how to leave the dark night sky" shows he true thoughts of her life as she made her place of work by overcoming difficulties for several years, just as she stated in the preface.

In the fourth paragraph, "Now, / the wind flaps the skirt, / and the hot sun undresses you, so / Eve, open your eyes" the poet explains that everything should be cared for and loved for the "For the fruits of the coming autumn."

The mission, and perhaps the only mission, for poets is to prepare and perfect poems. It may be more correct to say that poets receive poems, rather than creating poems. At all

일순간마다 시의 영원회귀에 참여한다. 시인은 오랜 여정을 통해 고정된 삶의 틀을 깨고 지각과 언어의 쇄신을 이룩한다.

아무리 가려도 걷어낸다
아랫도리는 멋대로 밖으로 뛰쳐나온다.
바람에 나부끼는 폭넓은 깃발
나의 부끄러움을 모른다

치맛바람 펄럭일 때마다
오므렸다 펴졌다 하는 펄럭이는 쾌감
신이 내려준 나의 만족이다

때로는 찢겨지고 닳아버리는
손수건보다 못하지만
돛단배에 매달린 깃발처럼
내가 항해하는 바다 같기도 하다

차라리 벗어 버리면 좋으련만
나를 풍요롭게 하는 치마
아름답게 펄럭인다.

－「치마」 전문

시인은 여성성을 강조하고 있다. 이 시집의 제명題名에서부터 나타나듯이 시인은 잠잠하지만 심연에서 이는 소용돌이 같은 자긍심과 사회적으로 부딪치는 표면의

times, poets participate in the eternal recurrence of poems. Poets break out of a fixed lifestyle through long journeys and achieve a reform of perception and words.

> No matter how much I cover it, it skims,
> the bottom runs outside,
> the wide flag that flutters in the wind,
> it knows not my shyness.
>
> Whenever my skirt flutters,
> the joy of the fluttering that puckers and spreads,
> it is my satisfaction given by god.
>
> Sometimes it rips and becomes worn out,
> and it is no better than a handkerchief,
> like a flag hung on a sailboat,
> it is like the sea that I navigate.
>
> It might be nicer to just take it off,
> but the skirt makes me fuller,
> and it flutters beautifully.
>
> - 'Skirt'

This poet emphasizes femininity. As apparent in the title of this collection of poems, the poet displays a maelstrom-like pride that occurs in a quiet abyss and the will to fiercely resist and overcome

장력을 완강히 저항하며 이겨나가는 의지를 보여주고 있다. 시의 제목처럼 "치마"는 여성성의 상징이다. "아무리 가려도 걷어낸다/아랫도리는 멋대로 밖으로 뛰쳐나온다/바람에 나부끼는 폭넓은 깃발/나의 부끄러움을 모른"다고 이 시 첫 연에서부터 여성으로서의 한계를 극복하려는 강렬한 의지를 보여준다. 결국 "때로는 찢겨지고 닳아버리는/손수건보다 못하지만/돛단배에 매달린 깃발처럼/내가 항해하는 바다 같기도 하다"고 소리치면서 끝 연에서는 "차라리 벗어 버리면 좋으련만/나를 풍요롭게 하는 치마/아름답게 펄럭"이는 자긍심의 상징으로서 아름다움을 강조하고 있다. 여기서 그의 시적 세계를 이루어 가는 과정을 이해할 수 있는 것이다. 좋은 시를 맞이하기 위해서는 항상 간절함을 가지고 있어야 한다.

긴 겨울 외투 하나 없이 찬비 맞으며
아무리 나의 상흔을 어루만져도
지워지지 않는 육신

가냘픈 엄마는 내 곁에서 울어도
쉽지 않은 칙칙한 장마만
침실을 메운다.

어머니의 입가에는 주름이 잡혀도
입김으로 호호 불어주던 사랑은
나의 가슴에 움츠렸던 생명이 피어난다

the surface tensions that she faces in society. The title of the poem 'skirt' is a symbol of femininity. "No matter how much I cover it, it skims, / the bottom runs outside, / the wide flag that flutters in the wind, / it knows not my shyness." The first paragraph of this poem shows the strong will to overcome the limitations of a woman. She ultimately cries out "Sometimes it rips and becomes worn out, / and it is no better than a handkerchief, / like a flag hung on a sailboat, / it is like the sea that I navigate." And at the end of the poem, she emphasizes beauty as the symbol of pride saying "It might be nicer to just take it off, / but the skirt makes me fuller, / and it flutters beautifully." Here, it is possible to understand the process that creates her poetic world. In order to meet good poems, one must always have a sense of desperateness.

> Being hit by cold rain without one coat in the long winter,
> no matter how much my wounds are cared for,
> the body does not erase.
>
> Even if my feeble mother cries next to me,
> the difficult and gloomy monsoon
> fills my room.
>
> Even if there are wrinkles around the mouth of my mother,
> the love she blew into me
> gives birth to life in my bosom.

먹구름 지나고 흐르는 신비의 서광
나의 구석구석 밝혀주셨던 정성
지금 내가 다시 어머니가 된다.

-「투병 속의 어머니 손길」 전문

여성성은 결과적으로 모성성과 직결된다. 모성은 신성하기까지 하며 끊임없이 나를 찾는 근원이기도 하다. 우리 문학에서 나타나는 모성성은 태초의 어머니로서의 상징성, 본능성, 탄생성, 지혜로운 어머니상, 자기희생의 모습 등으로 그려져 있다. 모성은 이렇듯 신화나 민담 등을 통해서 사회에서 원하는 모습으로서의 여성을 그려왔다. 즉, 사회에서 바라는 여성다움이란 수동성이나 기원하는 자세, 인내, 자기희생, 모성성 같은 것으로 범주화되어 오게 된 것이다. 인용하는 시 「투병 속의 어머니 손길」은 병고에 시달리는 어머니에 대한 회상이며 시인이 어머니로서의 자각을 나타내기도 한다. "어머니의 입가에는 주름이 잡혀도/입김으로 호호 불어주던 사랑은/나의 가슴에 움츠렸던 생명이 피어난"다는 3연은 이를 여실히 말해준다. 이어 끝 연에서는 "먹구름 지나고 흐르는 신비의 서광/나의 구석구석 밝혀주셨던 정성/지금 내가 다시 어머니가 된"다는 시적 화자 자신의 모성에 대한 자각을 고백한다.

일반적으로 여성은 생산자로서의 역할을 다하며, 모성

A mysterious sign that flows after the dark clouds,
the devotion that brightened every corner of my body,
I now become a mother.

- 'Mother's Touch in Sickness'

Ultimately, femininity is directly connected to maternity. Maternity is almost holy and it is the source of always finding one's self. Maternity in our literature is depicted through symbols of the first mother, instinct, birth, ideal of wise mothers, and self sacrifice. Maternity was depicted in the image desired by society through myths and legends. In other words, femininity seen by society was categorized as passiveness, attitude of prayer, patience, self-sacrifice and maternity. The poem 'Mother's Touch in Sickness' is a reminiscence of her mother who was sick and also displays the poet's self-perception as a mother. The third paragraph, "Even if there are wrinkles around the mouth of my mother, / the love she blew into me / gives birth to life in my bosom" shows this clearly. The last paragraph, "A mysterious sign that flows after the dark clouds, / the devotion that brightened every corner of my body, / I now become a mother" confesses her self-perception of her maternity.

Generally, women play the role of a producer and are demanded an identity of maternity. Such perceptions are spread to everybody through literature and creates a conception that maternity as a natural

을 정체성으로 가지기를 강요받게 되고, 그런 인식들이 문학을 통해서 모든 사람들에게 전해지게 되면서 모성이 본능이라는 의식을 하게 되는 것이다. 그러므로 모성을 가지지 못한 여성은 비판받게 되고 사회적 주체성을 얻지 못하게 된다. 『장화홍련전』, 『콩쥐팥쥐』, 『사씨남정기』 등의 계모형 소설이나 민담을 통해서 반 모성을 비판하고, 여성이 모성을 지니는 것이 당연시되고 있다.

사랑으로 엮을 줄 알았던 새끼줄이
이렇게 고독한 끈이 될 줄이야
마디마디 질시의 눈을 매달아 놓고
울타리에 걸쳐 놓는다

검은 눈이 내린다
공해에 찌든 삶이 베여있는 눈은
황토물처럼 금방 녹아내린다

－「서러운 인연」 부분

누구나 인연을 소중하게 여긴다. 불교에서는 모든 것이 생기 하거나 소멸하는 데는 반드시 원인이 있다고 보고, 생멸에 직접 관계하는 것을 인이라고 하며, 인을 도와서 결과를 낳는 간접적인 조건을 연으로서 구별하는데, 실제로 무엇이 인이고 무엇이 연인가를 확실히 구분하는 기준이 있는 것은 아니다. 인연은 '인과 연' 과 '인

instinct. Therefore, women without maternity are criticized and do not attain a social identity. Novels or folklores on evil stepmothers such as 'A Tale of Two Sisters', 'Kongjwi, Patjwi' and 'Sassi-Namjeonggi' criticizes anti-maternity and makes it only natural for women to have maternity.

> This straw rope that I thought would tie with love,
> I knew not that it would become such a lonely string.
> Eyes of jealousy are tied on each knot
> and placed on a fence.
>
> Black snow falls.
> The snow containing the life tainted with pollution
> melts quickly like mud.
>
> - Excerpt from 'Sad Relationship'

Relationships are important to everyone. Buddhism says that there is a reason for all things that are come into being and that cease to exist. Relationship, or *in-yeon*, in Buddhism is explained by '*in*', which is directly related to existence and non-existence, and '*yeon*' that is an indirect condition that helps '*in*' to create results. But there is no criteria to clearly separate what is '*in*' and what is '*yeon*'. *Inyeon* is interpreted either as '*in* and *yeon*' and '*yeon* through *in*'. The two are summed up and called *inyeon* and the act of giving life

으로서의 연'의 두 가지로 해석되는데, 이 양자를 일괄해서 인연이라고 하며, 인연에 의해서 사물이 생기 하는 것을 연기緣起라고 하며, 발생한 결과를 포함해서 '인과'라고도 한다. 이 시의 시적 화자 역시 첫 연에서 "사랑으로 엮을 줄 알았던 새끼줄이/이렇게 고독한 끈이 될 줄이야/마디마디 질시의 눈을 매달아 놓고/울타리에 걸쳐 놓는"다고 '서러운 인연'을 노래한다.

아침마다 쳐다보는 거울에
어머니가 없다

유달리 양 볼을 붉히던 다홍빛 모습
내 생각에 남아 있는데
거울을 보는 어머니의 옛 모습이 아니다

내 가슴에는 어머니 옛 모습
그대로 있었는데 거울 속을 아무리
찾아도 옛 어머니가 없다

–「어머니의 거울」 부분

이명희 시인의 첫 시집의 시적 이미지는 '사랑', '한', '업보'와 '현실에 대한 염원'과 '과거에 대한 회상'을 강렬하게 비치고 있다. 앞에 인용한 「어머니의 거울」도 어머니에 대한 사랑과 한스러움과 돌이켜봄을 통해 자신 속에 머물러 있는 어머니의 모습을 증폭시킨다. "아

through such relationship, or *inyeon*, is called *yeongi*, and everything including the results that occurred are called '*ingwa*'. The poet also sings of a 'sad relationship' in the first paragraph saying, "This straw rope that I thought would tie with love, / I knew not that it would become such a lonely string. / Eyes of jealousy are tied on each knot / and placed on a fence.

In the mirror I look at every morning,
mother is not there.

Her scarlet cheeks,
still remain in my memory,
but it is not what my mother looked like in the past.

My mother's image in the past,
it was still there, but no matter how hard I look,
my mother is not in the mirror.

- Excerpt from 'Mother's Mirror'

The poetic image of Myung Hee Lee's first book of poems strongly reflects 'love', 'resentment', 'karma', 'wishes for reality' and 'reminiscence of the past'. The citation from 'Mother's Mirror' also amplifies the image of her mother that she retains by looking back at her love and resentment to her mother. "In the mirror I look at every morning, / mother is not there" explains her continuous

침마다 쳐다보는 거울에/어머니가 없"다며 어머니의 모성애에 대한 회상은 끝없이 이어지는 것이다.

도심은 공해의 물결이다
지나가는 위선의 겸손으로
권력을 잡으려는
험난한 장애물 경기

호기심 반
걱정 반
합하면 하나지만
줄곧 도심은 몸살을 앓는다
편안한 곳 못 찾아
나도 몸살을 앓는다.

—「도심의 물결」 부분

오늘날 인류의 과학기술은 눈부시게 발전했지만, 한편으로는 위험성을 간직하고 있기도 하다. 하이데거에 따르면 현대의 기술문명은 인간이 자신을 주체라고 자부하는 가운데 존재 자체가 가장 철저하게 망각되어 있고 존재 자체가 이렇게 망각됨으로써 존재가 자신을 지배에의 맹목적인 의지로서 왜곡된 형태로 고지하고 있는 시대이다. 흔히 현대는 인간성 상실의 암흑시대라고 일컫기도 한다.

현대 사회의 도심지는 각종 공해와 생태계 파괴로 인

reminiscence of the maternal love of her mother.

The city is a wave of pollution.
With humility of passing hypocrisy,
a tough game
to gain power.

Half curious,
half worry,
the sum is one.
The city always suffers from aches.
Unable to find a place of refuge,
I am also filled with aches.

- Excerpt from 'Urban Waves'

Though science technology has developed greatly, it has on the other hand, risk. According to Heidegger, people proudly state that they are at the center of modern technological civilization as they completely forget existence itself. As existence itself is forgotten in this age, existence is being notified in a distorted format as a blinded will under the dominance of one's self. Typically, modernity is also called the dark ages of lost humanity.

Due to the growing damages caused by various pollutions and destruction of the ecology in urban societies and the dilution of social responsibilities and sense of ethics due to the decline of

한 폐해가 늘어나고 합리적 인간성의 퇴조로 사회적 책임과 윤리 의식이 희박해짐으로 인해 '탈 도심'을 부르짖는 사람들이 늘어나고 있다. 이 시의 시적 화자 역시 "도심은 공해의 물결이다/지나가는 위선의 겸손으로/권력을 잡으려는/험난한 장애물 경기"라고 진술하고 "편안한 곳 못 찾아/나도 몸살을 앓는"다는 스스로의 내면을 나타내고 있다.

밤이 두렵습니다
몹쓸 꿈속을 헤매게 될까
여명黎明이 영영 오지 못할까

밤이 두렵습니다
그대, 다른 정원에 서성여서
못 보게 되지나 않을까

밤이 두렵습니다
어두운 밤이
내 마음에 묻을까 두렵습니다.

—「잠 못 이루는 밤」 전문

문화와 역사는 밤에도 피어난다. 밤의 문화가 잠을 빼앗아 가는 현상이 확산하기도 하지만 분화와 심화를 거듭하는 밤의 추억처럼 밤은 문화를 만드는 아늑한 분위기를 애초부터 가지고 있다. 그러나 이명희 시인에겐

reasonable humanity, there are increasing number of people crying out for 'de-urbanization'. The poet also says, "The city is a wave of pollution. / With humility of passing hypocrisy, / a tough game / to gain power." She also expresses her inner self saying, "Unable to find a place of refuge, / I am also filled with aches."

I am afraid of the night.
Perhaps I will wander in a terrible dream,
Perhaps dawn will never come.

I am afraid of the night.
You, might pace around in another garden,
and I might not be able to see you.

I am afraid of the night.
Perhaps the dark night,
will close my heart.

- 'Sleepless Night'

Culture and history occurs in night as well. While the culture of night is increasingly robbing people of sleep, like the memories of night that repeats division and intensification, night also has a pleasant atmosphere that creates culture. But Myung Hee Lee says "I am afraid of the night. / Perhaps I will wander in a terrible dream,

"밤이 두렵습니다/몹쓸 꿈속을 헤매게 될까/여명黎明이 영영 오지 못할까"하고 잠 못 이루는 밤이 된다. 밤은 지난날들에 대한 회한, 앞날의 불확실성에 대한 두려움 등 추상적인 시간을 구상화한 것이 되기도 한다. 때에 따라서는 바느질하듯이, 그 긴긴 겨울밤을 옷감을 바느질하듯이 자기의 뜻으로 재구성한다. 긴 겨울밤의 허리를 베어내는 것이다. 그렇게 잘라낸 밤을 춘풍 이불 아래 서리서리 넣었다가 님이 오신 날 밤에는 굽이굽이 펴기도 한다. 기다림과 만남이 서로 대응하듯이 밤은 모순이다. 그런데 시인은 "밤이 두렵습니다/어두운 밤이/내 마음에 묻을까 두렵다"고 단정한다.

그 까닭은 "그대, 다른 정원에 서성여서/못 보게 되지나 않을"까 하는 우려 혹은 조바심이다.

쉴 곳 찾아 헤매다
낯선 골목에서
당신을 보았습니다

구부러진 골목은
애환과 정겨움이 땀 냄새와 어울려
삶의 옷깃을 적시고 있습니다

곧은길에 익숙한 세월
나의 영혼의 눈이 멀어
당신을 보지 못할까 걱정입니다.

/ Perhaps dawn will never come" and her nights become sleepless. Night is a visualization of abstract time such as past regrets and fear of future uncertainties. Sometimes like sewing, the long winter nights are reconstructed as one sees fit like sewing clothes. It is the act of cutting out the hip of the long winter nights. The nights that have been cut out are sometimes hidden away in winter blankets and then brought out when a lover comes at night. Just as waiting and meeting conflicts against each other, night is contradictory. But, the poet says "I am afraid of the night. / Perhaps the dark night, / will close my heart." The reason is concerns of "I am afraid of the night. / You, might pace around in another garden, / and I might not be able to see you."

In search for a place of rest,
in an unfamiliar alley,
I saw you.

In the bending alleys
sadness, happiness and affection mixes with the smell
of sweat
and soaks the collars of life.

The days spend on straight paths,
I am worried that the eyes of my soul goes blind
and that I might not be able to see you.

내 앞에 펼쳐진 골목 길
세상의 깊이와 넓이를 느끼며
당신 앞에 무거운 짐을 내려놓습니다.

-「애환哀歡의 길목에서」 전문

운명이란 무엇일까? 의문은 끝없이 번져가지만 확실한 답은 떠오르지 않고 그저 알 수 없는 사실에 마음 답답한 느낌이 들 뿐이다. 그렇지만 그 답답한 마음 한가운데로 애잔해지는 감정 한 자락을 갖게 되는 것은 이상한 일이다. "쉴 곳 찾아 헤매다/낯선 골목에서/당신을 보았"다는 시인은 많은 슬픔과 체념과 긍지와 초연함이 융합된 일생에서 스스로의 운명마저 보는 것 같아 설레고 두려운 말을 잃는다. "곧은길에 익숙한 세월/나의 영혼의 눈이 멀어/당신을 보지 못할까 걱정"이라는 시인은 살아오면서 기다림에 대한 설레임이 얼마나 깊고 충실한 것인지를 체감하면서 "내 앞에 펼쳐진 골목 길/세상의 깊이와 넓이를 느끼며/당신 앞에 무거운 짐을 내려놓는"다고 자신의 의지를 밝힌다. 막막한 세월을 보내고 이제 새로운 삶에 대한 성찰과 체득을 위한 실존적 자아로서의 대응 의지인 것이다.

TV 속이 썩었는지 드라마가 온통 제정신이 아니다.
예쁜 인형들은 각본의 글줄 따라
전부 탈선한다.

The alley in front of me,
feeling the depth and width of the world,
I rest my heavy burdens in front of you.

- 'At a Street Corner of Joys and Sorrows'

What is destiny? Though questions continue to spread, there is no clear answer and I feel stuffy with unknown facts. But strangely, I have a string of sympathy in such stuffiness. The poet says, "In search for a place of rest, / in an unfamiliar alley, / I saw you." She loses words in excitement and fear because she feels to see her destiny in daily life that combines many sadness, resignation, pride and aloofness. The paragraph, "The days spend on straight paths, / I am worried that the eyes of my soul goes blind / and that I might not be able to see you" shows how deep and loyal the excitement of waiting is in life. She then reveals her will saying, "The alley in front of me, / feeling the depth and width of the world, / I rest my heavy burdens in front of you." It is her will to react as a real person in order to part with the gloomy past and to reflect on herself and learn a new life.

Perhaps the TV is rotten, but dramas are out of their minds.
Pretty dolls follow the script
and all become erratic.

탈선의 경마장은 진흙투성이다
도덕과 윤리는 흰개미의 침입으로
썩어버린 통나무
어디까지 썩어야 할지 모른다

세대와 세대로 이어가는 고통이
언제 멈출지 모르는 형벌일까?

— 「TV 드라마」 부분

무료한 일상에서 벗어나기 위해 텔레비전 드라마에 매달리는 사람들을 본다. 텔레비전이 사람들에게 미치는 영향을 말하는 사람들도 많다. 반인륜적 반사회적 범죄가 일어날 때마다 범죄영화나 폭력영상물이 사회적 지탄을 받게 되고 텔레비전 드라마에 대한 시시비비도 일어나게 마련이다. 이 시에서도 텔레비전 드라마를 화두로 삼는다. 시적 화자는 "TV 속이 썩었는지 드라마가 온통 제정신이 아니다./예쁜 인형들은 각본의 글줄 따라/전부 탈선한"다며 텔레비전 드라마를 혐오한다. 그리고 "탈선의 경마장은 진흙투성이다/도덕과 윤리는 흰개미의 침입으로/썩어버린 통나무/어디까지 썩어야 할지 모른"다면서 텔레비전 드라마의 폐해에 대한 화두를 곱씹고 곱씹으며 부조리한 사회적 현실을 개탄한다. 시인이 포착한 텔레비전 드라마의 문제점은 "세대와 세대로 이어가는 고통"이면서 "언제 멈출지 모르는 형벌"이라고

The race track of deviation is filled with mud.
Morals and ethics are attacked by mites,
and a rotten piece of wood.
Nobody knows to where it will rot.

Pains that are passed down from one generation to the next,
is it punishment that nobody knows when it will stop?

- Excerpt from 'TV Drama'

Some people spend their time attached to TV dramas to escape from their humdrum lives. Many people talk about the effects of television on people. Whenever anti-human or anti-social crimes occur, crime movies or violence on television receive social criticism and there are always disputes over television dramas. This poet also talks about television dramas. The poet shows hatred against television dramas saying, "Perhaps the TV is rotten, but dramas are out of their minds. / Pretty dolls follow the script / and all become erratic." She also says "The race track of deviation is filled with mud. / Morals and ethics are attacked by mites, / and a rotten piece of wood. / Nobody knows to where it will rot" as she talks about the harms of television drama while complaining about the irrational social reality. She says that the problem with television drama is "Pains that are passed down from one generation to the next," and that it

단호하게 선을 긋는다. 시인은 시대의 대변자이기 때문에.

허망하게 걸어온 세월
되돌아갈 수 없어
모두가 한숨 되어 창가에 서리구나

창밖에는 새싹 파릇한데
어인 일로 자욱한 안개에
스며오는 어두움 뿐

햇빛이 강하면 그림자도 강한데
나는
육신과 그림자가 따로 노는구나

그림자가 나를 떠날 때
한 줌의 재가 될지
흙이 될지 모르지만

그때엔
기쁨도 슬픔도
허망할 마음조차 있을 수 없어라

–「망상妄想」 전문

시간의 흐름을 인식할 수 있을 때 인간은 동물적 단계에서 신적인 단계로 격상한다. 그것은 반성적 사유를 통

is "punishment that nobody knows when it will stop." This is because poets are the spokespersons of the eras.

> Times passed in vain,
> I cannot return to
> and turns into sighs and fogs up the window.
>
> Out of the window new shoots are green,
> but for some reason thick fogs,
> and a darkness that spreads.
>
> When the sun is strong so is its shadow,
> and I
> have a different body and shadow.
>
> When my shadow leaves me
> it may become a handful of ash
> or perhaps even dirt.
>
> At that time,
> no happiness and no sadness,
> not even a heart to have remorse for will be left.
>
> - 'Delusion'

When people recognize the flow of time, they are upgraded from animals to gods. This is because they can change meaningless life to a world of very noble and pure values through reflecting reasons.

해 무의미한 삶을 지고지순한 가치의 세계로 바꿀 수 있기 때문이다. 이 시에 나타나는 것은 지나온 삶의 여정에 대한 회상과 반성이다. 이 시의 첫 연 "허망하게 걸어온 세월/되돌아갈 수 없어/모두가 한숨 되어 창가에 서리구나"라는 구절은 이를 고백하는 시인의 회한이다. 이것은 무의미로 떨어져 가는 삶에 대한 반성적 인식의 표현인 것이다. "그때엔/기쁨도 슬픔도/허망할 마음조차 있을 수 없어"라는 마지막 연의 진술은 오랜 번민 끝에 진정한 실존이 어디에 있는지를 알게 되어 운명의 실타래를 이제야 여기서 만지는 듯한 느낌을 주고 있는 것이다.

이번에 간행되는 이명희 시인의 처녀 시집 『이브여, 눈을 뜨라』는 그동안의 현실에 얽매인 평범한 삶에서 시간의 흐름을 인식하고 한층 승화된 세계의 새로운 삶, 즉 자아의 아집을 이겨낸 우주적 자아로의 탄생, 공존공생하는 순응적 삶으로 변화하는 계기가 되었다고 하겠다.

시인이 순명을 통해 그의 시가 가닿는 지점은 시적 깊이와 넓이에 따라 거리가 달라질 것이다. "배는 항구에/머물러 있기 위해서 있는 것이 아니라/파도를 헤치며 항해를 하기 위함"이라고 시인이 노래했듯이 가벼워지고 낮아지며 자유로워짐으로 낮은 곳에 대한 사랑을 통해 진실과 긍정의 세계를 자각하면서 이명희 시인 특유의

This poem is about remorse and reflection on the past journeys of life.

The first paragraph, "Times passed in vain, / I cannot return to / and turns into sighs and fogs up the window" shows the remorse of the poet. This is an expression of reflective perception on life that is becoming more and more meaningless. "At that time, / no happiness and no sadness, / not even a heart to have remorse for will be left." This last paragraph expresses her finally touching the skein of destiny after learning where truth is through long times of anguish.

Myung Hee Lee's first collection of poems 'Eve, Open Your Eyes' was the opportunity to change the common life tied up with reality into a new life in an upgraded world by recognizing the flow of time, or in other words, her birth as a person of the space that overcame the obstinacy of the self and an adaptive life that coexists.

The point that her poems reach through obedience will differ depending on its poetic depth and width. Just as the poet sang, "A ship / Is meant to plow through the waves / Not to just stay still" she becomes lighter, lower and freer to perceive a world of truth and positivity through love from the lowest places. And thus, Lee should also newly open her own world of poetry.

It can be viewed that the poems of Lee recognizes and loves that she lived in this world, existed and thought in anguish, and left her

시 세계를 새롭게 열어가야 할 것이다.

결국, 이명희의 시는 시인이 이 세계에 살았음을, 고뇌하며 존재했음을, 그리고 이 세계 삼라만상에 또 하나의 의미 있는 발자취를 남겼음을 인정하고 사랑한 것으로 볼 수 있다.

이러한 점에서 그의 시는 존재의 운명을 확인하고 달래는 측면에서 순명의 사상이 가닿는 궁극의 지점에 뚜렷한 좌표가 될 것임은 불문가지다. 복잡하고 미묘한 이 실존적 세계에서 생의 본질과 운명을 성스러운 상태로 승화시키며 덧없는 사물에 미적 진리를 부여하는 시인으로서의 길을 초연하고 당당하게 걸어갈 것을 믿어본다.

traces in this world's nature.

From such point, her poems confirm and soothe the destiny of existence and will be clear coordinates in the ultimate point that the thought of obedience meets. I believe that in this complex and delicate real world, she will walk the path of a poet who sublimates the essence and destiny of life to a thing of holiness and grant aesthetic truth on objects.

이명희 시집

# 이브여, 눈을 뜨라

2014년 8월  8일 인쇄
2014년 8월 15일 발행
지은이 | 이명희
펴낸이 | 최장락
펴낸곳 | 도서출판 두손컴
부산광역시 부산진구 부전로 35 삼성B/D 301호
전화 : (051)805-8002 팩스 : (051)805-8045
이메일 : doosoncomm@hanmail.net
출판등록 제329-1997-13호


값 20,000원
* 저자와 협의에 의해 인지를 생략합니다.

The Collection of Myung Hee Lee's Poems

# EVE, OPEN YOUR EYES

Printed on Aug 8, 2014
Published on Aug 15, 2014
Author | Myung Hee Lee
Publisher | Jang Rak Choi
Publishing Co. | Doosoncomm Publishing Co.
301 Samsung Bldg, 35, Bujeon-ro,
Busanjin-gu, Busan, Korea (Postal Code : 614-850)
Telephone : 82-51)805-8002 Facsimile : 82-51)805-8045
E-mail : doosoncomm@hanmail.net
Registration No. : 329-1997-13


Price : ₩20,000
* Damaged books are to be exchanged.

ISBN 978-89-97083-99-2-03810

이 도서의 국립중앙도서관 출판시도서목록(CIP)은 서지정보유통지원시스템 홈페이지(http://seoji.nl.go.kr)와 국가자료공동목록시스템(http://www.nl.go.kr/kolisnet)에서 이용하실 수 있습니다.(CIP제어번호: CIP2014023202)